The Creative Violinist

The Creative Violinist

Integrating Technique and
Music through Improvisation

Christopher N. Brooks

Orpheus

ISBN: 978-0-9892206-0-6

"A system of proportions in the service of spiritual impulse."
-The composer George Crumb's definition of music

TABLE OF CONTENTS

Introduction: How to use this book

FOR WHOM IS IT WRITTEN?

This book is written for violin and viola students (and their teachers) who would benefit from integrating musicianship and technique through improvisation. The focus is on what might be called intermediate players, though it can be used to teach beginners who have at least a basic ability to hold and play the instrument. For the sake of brevity, the discussion is cut off at the level of virtuoso technique and complicated jazz improvisation.

This creative approach to musical elements and technique should help improve facility and expression for written music; empower participation with other musicians playing in improvisation-based approaches such as blues, country, or rock; and even provide a springboard to dive into the deep waters of jazz.

Throughout the book, I assume some knowledge of musical terminology. If the student does not have the vocabulary, a teacher should be able to explain. I found that writing specifically in terms of the violin helped focus my thinking. But violists, 'cellists, and other instrumentalists can also benefit from this book, particularly since the written musical examples are intended to clarify concepts, rather than as exercises to be read from the page. My hope is that copies of this book will become dog-eared and coffee-stained from much use.

This book is meant to be a tool, rather than to be read from left to right, cover to cover.
Use a pencil and scrawl all over it.

HOW IS IT ORGANIZED?

Following this introduction are eleven chapters exploring basic musical and technical concepts:

1. Pitch (scales)
2. Rhythm (time)
3. Dynamics
4. Left hand
5. Right hand
6. Melody
7. Harmony and form
8. Accompaniment
9. Ensemble
10. Intonation
11. Resources (tools, books, etc.)

Each of these chapters contains a short discussion of the concept (some with fundamental physical exercises), followed by a list of "parameters" for creative exploration, roughly in ascending order of difficulty. As you work through the book, mark with a pencil to track your progress (though backtracking to review may also be fruitful). Each of these parameters is a defined set of musical elements, or a concept, to be used as the basis for work and exploration, including improvisation.

Of course, all of these concepts are completely interrelated. For example, most work focusing on rhythm will involve the right hand (though a lot can be accomplished with clapping or using a drum); most work in the realm of pitch will use the left hand; melody relates to harmony; all playing involves dynamics, etc. As will be explained below, these parameters can be combined for creative exploration.

HOW TO USE THIS BOOK

Many books on music technique contain long lists of exercises to be practiced with permutations of bowings, rhythms, patterns, and transpositions. Readers may be familiar with the Galamian scale method, the Sevcik methods, or Patterns for Jazz (see *Chapter 11: Resources*). The problem that I always had with these methods is that the number of possible permutations is overwhelming; one could practice forever without leaving the first page.

This book organizes the excellent concept of playing with permutations by using flashcards (back page). In contrast with the methods cited above, permutations are used as the basis for creative musical exploration: "playing" in its several senses.

If read as you would a novel, this book would be awfully dense. But if you jump to where you are working and keep track by marking with a pencil (not a pen!), it should be pretty straightforward. I heartily encourage my readers to scrawl all over the pages.

The process

Here is a suggested approach; others are certainly possible.

1. Pick a flashcard for your tonic note (unless you are going to work without notes).

2. Pick a flashcard for a number and open to the chapter with that number. Or you may wish to focus on a technical or musical area that has come up in performance or practicing for performance.

3. In the chosen chapter, choose the parameter that is next up on the list.

4. You may wish to add a parameter from another chapter (more than two can get cumbersome). For example, you may explore additive rhythms (from *Chapter 2: Rhythm*) with a bouncing bow (from *Chapter 5: Right Hand*), or explore shifting (from *Chapter 4: Left Hand*) with the Lydian mode (from *Chapter 1: Pitch*). Of course all of these elements are interrelated, so you can't avoid mixing them. Those elements that are undefined by the parameters are left free.

5. Using these parameters, explore. First, play the material in a straightforward fashion. For example, if the parameter is an Eb major scale in fourth position, play the scale up and down. Get comfortable with the material. Play very, very slowly. (Most students do not practice anywhere near slowly enough.)

6. Now start to explore. Create music within the constraints of the parameter (or parameters). Following our example, create melodies using only the notes of the Eb major scale in fourth position.

7. As you grow more comfortable with the elements of the parameter, push the boundaries: experiment with wider leaps or faster tempi, or add parameters from other chapters. For example, stay with the same pitch set (or scale) and work through several other parameters (rhythm, dynamics, phrase lengths).

8. You may wish to finish by relaxing the constraints and playing relatively freely, just following your intuition.

9. I often end a practice session with playing some repertoire that I know, or with a totally free improvisation.

10. You may want to stay with one set of parameters for several days. Or discard one that doesn't really seem to work, and move on.

The goal is not to play every single permutation. This is simply not possible. The goal is to explore fundamental musical elements in order to create expressive, meaningful, beautiful music. Record yourself often. Sometimes it helps to listen to your recording a day or so later. You will be surprised at the difference between your perception while playing, and later as an impartial listener.

Flashcards

I use flashcards to address the following issues:

o There is always more to practice than can be covered in one day. How do you keep track of what you need to work on, making sure that you don't neglect important material, over a longer period of time?

o Permutations and combinations of various elements can provide useful items to practice and as a basis for improvisation. However, the number of possible combinations is, essentially, infinite. How do you choose what to do at any one time?

The flashcards provided with the book function in four ways:

1. They have each of the twelve chromatic notes, so you rotate among all the keys.

2. Each note has frequencies for entering into tone-generating software to produce drones for practice.

3. The numbers can be used to choose a chapter.

4. The numbers can be used to choose numbered elements, such as which position, how many subdivisions of the beat, number of beats in a measure, etc.

You may also wish to make up your own flashcards, for instance to keep track of repertoire. Some repertoire you never want to leave behind, but it is not necessary to work on it every single day. For example, I have a set of flashcards in my violin case with every movement of the Bach Solo Sonatas. It may take over a year before I return again to a movement. But each time I do return, I take it to a higher level. (There is no limit with these pieces.)

THOUGHTS ON PRACTICING

o Your highest practicing priority should be material for upcoming performances.

o Perform as much as possible.

o Most of the time (not all) practice with a metronome.

o It is often helpful to set the metronome a little fast, then ratchet the tempo *downward* step by step. This approach is helpful for the tendency that most of us (not all) have to rush.

o Most of the time (not all), practice slowly. Sometimes, very, very slowly, much slower than you might think.

o Always play in tune. Playing with a drone is extremely helpful. See *Chapter 11: Resources* for freeware programs for playing tones. See the flashcards for frequencies.

o Always play with a beautiful tone.

o Focus on what you are actually playing, rather than on your judgment of what you are playing. It is helpful to distinguish between self-awareness (what is actually happening) and self-consciousness (what people think about what is happening). Aim for self-awareness.

o Monitor tension, particularly in the neck and shoulders. It's great if you can relax tension while playing. But if tension persists, stop completely, relax, take a deep breath, then return.

o Don't try to cover all the material that you are working on in one day; it's better to keep rotating material. The entire cycle may take many days. You may leave off a project for a period of time and return to find that it has improved as if on its own.

o In every practice session, something should change: whatever you are working on, something should be better than when you started. It is preferable to work on one thing for an entire practice session and improve it than to merely cover lots of material.

o It is better to practice many shorter sessions during the day than all at once, though not everyone has that luxury.

o Always return to old friends: pieces, tunes, ideas, chord progressions.

o There is much to be learned from "easy" material.

o Everyone, even complete beginners, should be able to perform *something* (it doesn't have to be difficult) at a moment's notice, without advance preparation. Fiddle tunes make great repertoire for this purpose.

All of the parameters are to be played with intent, expression, drama, and beauty. They are intended to be miniature pieces of music. So how do you do this?

I can only speak from personal experience. For example, it has never worked for me to "play like the color purple" or "play something happy, or sad." For me, it is all about the music itself.

So, here are my recommendations:

o Listen intently, primarily to people you are playing with (if you are) and to yourself, particularly your sound.

o Open your heart to what is being played. You have to consciously remind yourself to do this.

o Play with the full intention of the music you are playing now. The distilled expression of this music is the sound itself.

o Apply these rules to everything you play, starting with the material in this book.

Very few problems in music cannot be resolved by playing softer and listening harder.

Chapter 1: Pitch

THOUGHTS

There is a large overlap between this chapter and *Chapter 4: Left Hand,* which focuses more on the physical aspect of playing. This one focuses more on the notes, including fingering.

Even beginners should be able to play in all keys, and should get up into the positions as soon as possible (shifting between them comes next). Get up there and play! Reading facility in the positions (which is a little trickier) can catch up.

Playing in higher positions has many benefits:

o It makes proper position imperative. It is much more natural, for example, to play with a proper wrist position in fourth position.

o It requires finer attention to note spacing, and thus benefits intonation.

o It requires finer attention to the bow's distance from the bridge, and thus benefits tone production.

o It is easier to shift between positions because the thumb stays in one place.

o Students may appreciate the fact that it looks cool.

While playing in higher positions, always be aware of the relationship between what you are playing and the open strings. Harmonics of the open strings can help you do this.

Intonation

Chapter 10: Intonation, Tuning, and, Temperaments discusses the theory behind intonation in depth. Here is a practical overview:

o There is a difference between hearing intervals in terms of *harmony* (vertically) and in terms of *melodic* tendencies (horizontally). In harmonic intonation, major intervals tend not to be quite so wide, minor intervals not quite so narrow. By contrast, melodic tendencies, particularly leading tones, tend to exaggerate these intervals. For example, an F# played simultaneously with D as a major third (heard *harmonically*), would be lower than an F# as a leading tone to G (heard *melodically*).

o Equal temperament, used on keyboard and electronic instruments, is an artificial, but useful, compromise between these two tendencies.

This may sound complex (well, it is). It is true that, in practice, musicians get along quite well with listening for what sounds in tune. However, knowledge of these distinctions can be a tremendous help. I speak from personal experience.

WHAT TO DO

Pick a tonic note from the flashcards. At first, work with an open-string tonic (G, D, A, E). Then move to scales that contain open-string notes (for major scales: C, F, Bb, Eb, Ab, B). Finally, work on those remaining that contain no open-string notes at all (for example, F#, C# major scales).

When you can play in every single key, do so by picking any card at random from the stack.

With all the parameters listed below, follow the steps below. At every opportunity check notes against open strings, against harmonics, or work with a drone (see Software, page 119 for a sources for drones and the flashcards for frequencies).

Play very slowly from note to note up and down the scale.

1. **Meander:** in other words, go up a few steps, back down, up, down—all stepwise. In this way you can explore each of the notes and the relationships between them. Don't worry if it is working musically (yet)---though tone and intonation should always be excellent. See Figure 1 below.

Figure 1

2. Once you are comfortable, allow a leap every once in a while. Try if possible to always follow a leap with a step in the opposite direction (at least at first). Take pauses. Play phrases (don't worry if they are good, just play and listen).

3. Dig deep and play, within the parameter, as sensitively and musically as possible. Think of phrases as sentences, with breaths in between. Remember to open your heart to what you play, and breathe. Best if you can perform for someone.

4. After you are really comfortable with the notes, you can bring in parameters from other chapters (e.g., play in four-bar phrases from *Chapter 2: Rhythm*, use bouncing bow, etc.)

Always practice scales by memory. The examples n this chapter are provided as models from which to construct scales in all keys—without reading.

Single octave major scale

All scales up an octave and back down to tonic note.

1. Scales based on the open strings: open string up to third finger an octave above. Use open string on the way up, fourth finger on the way down (this is a general principle).

2. Start first finger, up to fourth on next higher string.

3. Start second finger, up to first two strings higher.

4. Start third finger, up to second two strings higher.

5. Start fourth finger, up to third two strings higher.

All positions, no shifting

Pick a position by choosing a flashcard for a number. Start with 1 through 4, but as soon as you can, go as high as twelfth position. It may seem scary up there, but by sticking within a single octave, and (at first) staying with open-string scales, you will find it very doable. Just play slowly enough so that you can make a good sound.

1. One-octave scale in a single position. Find the tonic note by relating to an open string.

2. All notes in the key in that position. In other words, all the notes within that scale, starting from first finger on the G string up to fourth finger on the E, without changing positions. The first finger on the G string will not necessarily be the tonic of the scale.

Shifting

For fingering scales that involve shifting, follow two rules:

1. Shift on half steps.

2. Avoid half steps across strings.

Follow these simple principles for all scales (including the more advanced ones) below and you will never need to buy a scale book.

In all the examples, fingerings are only notated where there is a shift, or where the fingering would be ambiguous. A parenthesis indicates an extension, without shifting.

The physical aspects of shifting are addressed in *Chapter 4: Left Hand.*

One octave, one string

Using your tonic note, start with first finger, and play a major scale up and down one octave using the following fingering: 1 2 3, 1 2 3 4 4 (extension). All shifts are on a half step. Do this on all four strings. The octave and position of your tonic note will be different for each one.

Figure 2

Three-octave scales

The G major scale starts on the open G string.

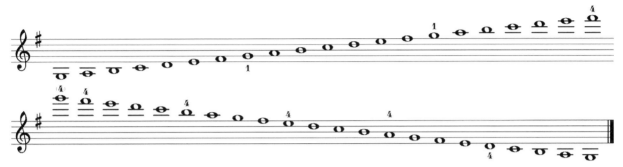

Figure 3

All other three-octave scales start on the first finger on the G string. In this way, you can follow the shifting rules, using the same fingering for all scales, both up and down

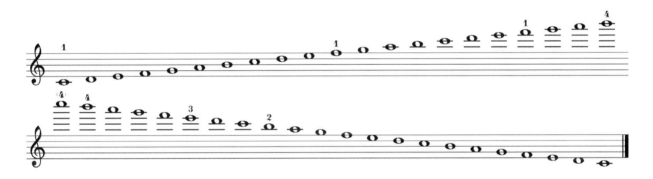

Figure 4

Melodic minor scales

Follow the same principles for three-octave melodic minor scales. Starting on open G:

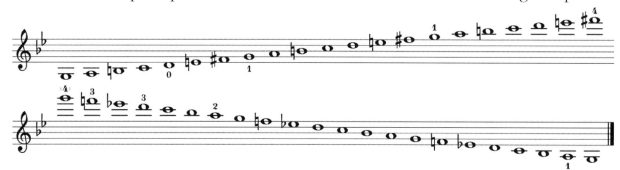

Figure 5

All others:

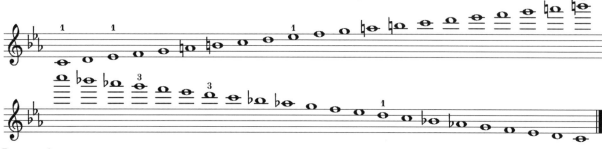

Figure 6

Modes

Modes are a wonderful source of material for improvisation. Playing against a drone brings out the characteristics of each mode (see *Software*, page 119, for sources for drones).

The acronym **LIMDAPL** (used at the Berklee College of Music) is a way of remembering the names of the modes in order.

o Lydian

o Ionian

o Mixolydian

o Dorian

o Aeolian

o Phrygian

o Locrian

This may seem complex, but the concept is simple: using the same tonic note, adjust the key signature. As you move to the next mode on the **LIMDAPL** sequence, subtract a sharp or add a flat. One way to think about this is that you modulate downward by a fifth, keeping the same tonic as you move through the sequence. In the examples below, the key signatures are listed with a C tonic (see Figure 7, below).

1. Play each mode by itself following the procedure for major scales discussed above.
2. Single octave first position.
3. Single octave in other positions.
4. Single octave up and down a single string, using the fingerings in Figure 7.

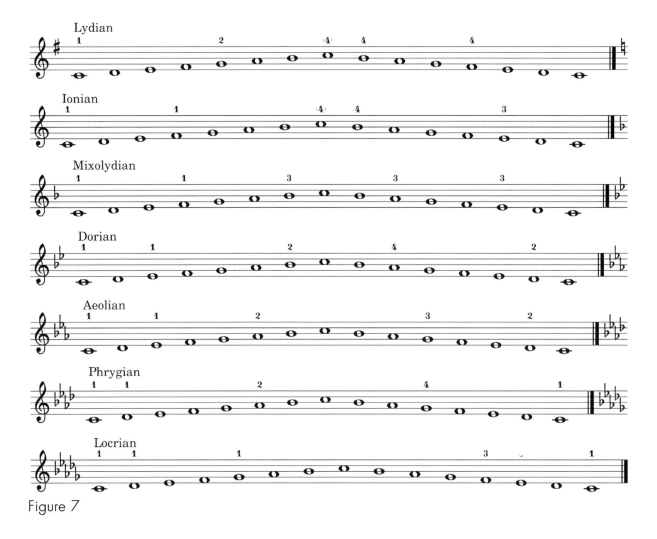

Figure 7

All shifts are on half steps. Note that the set of three whole steps in a row (which occurs in every mode) can be awkward, mandating shifts after the fourth finger. You may wish to experiment with breaking the half-step rule, playing 1 2, 1 2, rather than 1 2 3 4.

20

Play three octaves, following the two fingering principles.

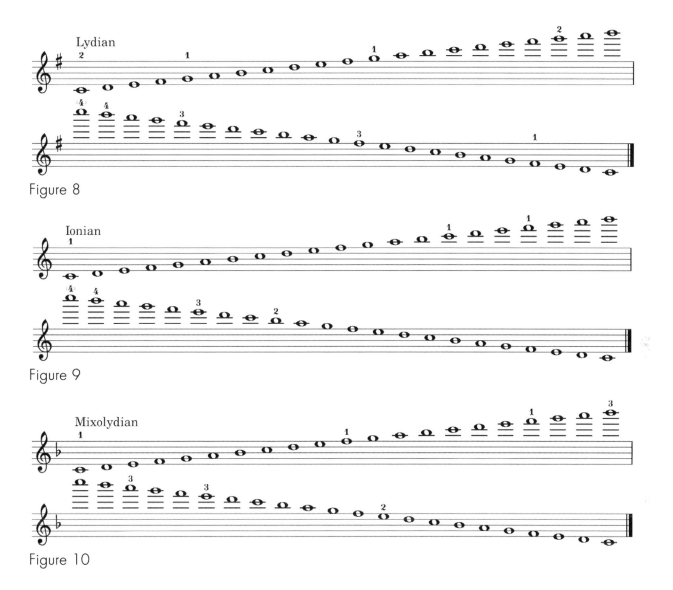

Figure 8

Figure 9

Figure 10

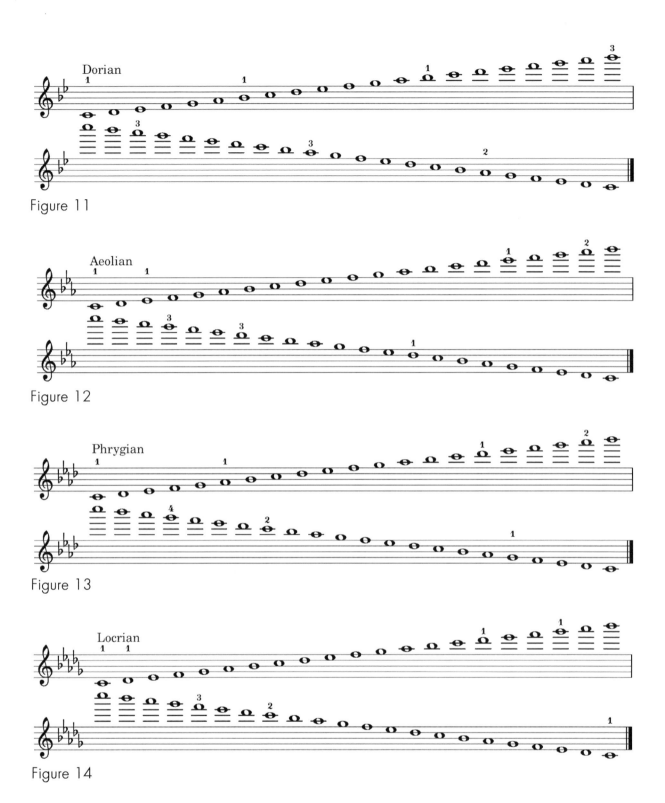

Figure 11

Figure 12

Figure 13

Figure 14

Play through the LIMDAPL sequence one mode after the other to get a sense of

how the changing key signatures creating shifting tonalities.

22

Once you are comfortable with them, use the modes to explore and improvise, as discussed at the beginning of the chapter.

More advanced scales

These scales are worth exploring, even for less advanced students, providing the opportunity to explore unorthodox fingerings and harmonies.

Start in the first position to give you some grounding. These scales are hard to hear. Play slowly. Have patience with yourself. Don't spend *too* much time on them. You can always return to them later.

Lydian Dominant scale

This scale is used extensively in jazz. It is also known as the Acoustic Scale, because all of its members can be found in the overtone series of the tonic. It implies a dominant harmony. (See *Chapter 6: Melody* and *Chapter 7: Harmony and Form*.)

Approach this scale in the same way you approach the modes. Once you are comfortable with them, you may wish to include this scale as one of the modes. It works nicely as the first, before Lydian.

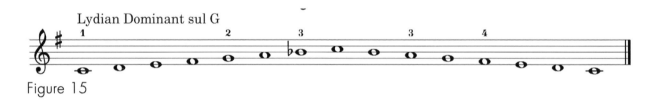

Figure 15

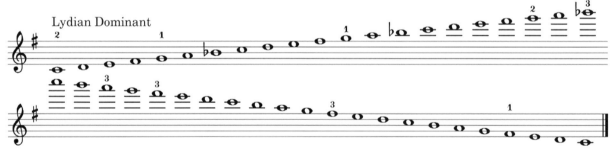

Figure 16

Tonally ambiguous scales: diminished and whole tone

These scales are tricky because they are tonally ambiguous and their fingerings are unorthodox. For example, the whole tone scale has no half steps to shift on. In both, one tends to move out of position across the fingerboard while moving up and down the scale.

The ambiguous tonality means that the choices of starting and ending notes are arbitrary and also makes the choice of accidentals ambiguous.

Diminished scale

The diminished scale alternates half and whole steps. There are three possible diminished scales, but since the scale is totally symmetrical, any note in the scale can be considered its tonic.

If a tonic note is chosen that is the lower member of a half-step pair, the scale can imply a dominant harmony. A diminished scale contains all the notes of two dominant chords with roots a tritone apart (e.g., C dominant + F# dominant + Eb Ab).

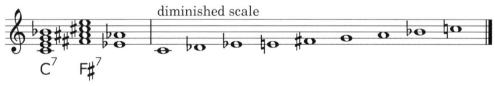

Figure 17

Diminished scales have eight notes plus the octave, as opposed to seven plus the octave in all the scales discussed so far. Choosing fingerings can be addressed in either of two ways:

1. Use the open strings as an extra finger.

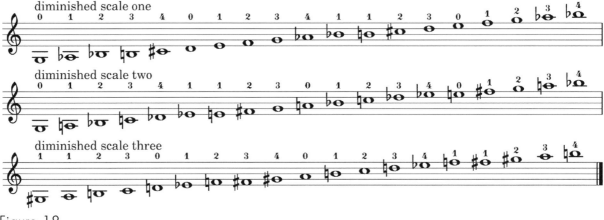

Figure 18

2. Move lower in the fingerboard (away from your nose) as you move from lower to higher strings. Chose a fingering with a half step between first and second finger so that there is a whole step between open strings.

To shift higher in the positions, play whole steps 1 2, 1 2, etc., shifting on the half steps. On the way down, use 2 1, 2 1, or 4 3 2 1. The same finger pattern can be used to travel as far up and down as you like.

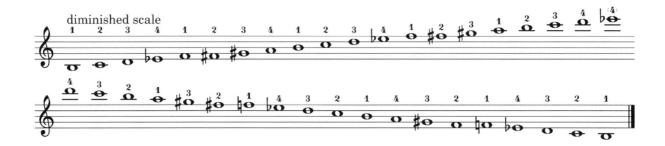

Figure 19

Whole tone scale

Like the diminished scale, the whole tone scale is tonally ambiguous. It is composed of all whole steps, resulting in six notes plus the octave. This means that playing upward, one moves up by a half-step position while moving from a lower string to a higher string.

There are only two possible whole tone scales and any note can be considered the tonic. Like the diminished scale, the whole tone scale can be used as a dominant harmony, since it contains the root, third and seventh of the dominant chord.

Whole tone scales automatically satisfy the rule to avoid half steps across strings and make it impossible to satisfy the rule to shift on half steps.

Figure 20

Double stops

Any violinist with a feel for the fingerboard and the ability to shift will benefit from practicing double stops. Practice mostly slowly. It is helpful to slur from pair of notes to pair of notes in order to practice the connection. Double stops are an excellent means to clarify the difference between harmonic and melodic intonation.

Fingering

Unlike for scales, fingerings for double stops are relatively straightforward.

o Sixths: For lower positions: alternating 0 1, 1 2, 2 3, 3 4. Use open strings whenever possible. Use 2 3, 2 3, 2 3, etc., for moving up and down the positions.

o Thirds: For lower positions: alternating 2 0, 3 1, 4 2. Use open strings whenever possible, alternating 1 3, 2 4 for moving up and down the positions.

o Octaves, artificial harmonics, tenths: 0 3 (when possible) and 1 4 all the way. Work on double stops in this order:

1. Thirds

2. Octaves

3. Artificial harmonics (excellent for setting the frame of the hand, bow control and intonation)

4. Once you are comfortable, tenths (fingering 1 4). The advantage of studying tenths is that it requires a good frame of the hand, centered on the fourth finger, with the first finger reaching back.

I am not a fan of fingered octaves. Some will disagree, but I find they cramp the hand and are not terribly useful.

Tartini Tones

Tartini Tones are a third, lower tone that occurs when two notes of a consonant interval are played in tune simultaneously. They are an invaluable tool for tuning double stops.[1]

interval	octave	fifth	fourth	major third	major sixth	minor third	minor sixth	major tenth	minor tenth
TT distance below lower note	unison	octave	fifth + octave	two octaves	fifth + two octaves	major third + two octaves	major sixth + two octaves	octave	major third + octave

Table 1

Another way to look at the same concept is shown in Figure 21 below. These are all intervals with the same Tartini Tone: the note played by the open G string.

Figure 21

---

[1] Brooks, Christopher. *The Third Way: The origin, reputation, and application of (say what?) Tartini Tones,* Strings Magazine, April 2008, 39.

Natural harmonics

Natural harmonics, played by placing the finger lightly on the string without pressing all the way to the fingerboard, are a fascinating way to explore the fundamentals of musical acoustics, to orient yourself high on the fingerboard, to encourage bow control, and as a source of material for improvisation. Figure 22, below, shows the natural harmonics organized in two ways:

1. One string at a time

2. In pitch order, creating a sort of scale

Because they go so high, the harmonics are notated an octave lower (that's what the 8 on top of the treble clef signifies).

Natural Harmonics in Low Positions

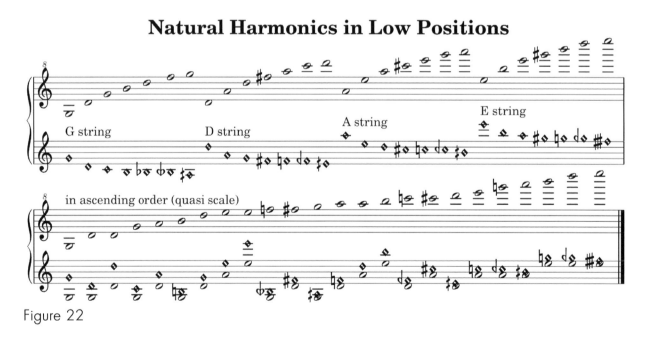

Figure 22

The highest harmonics (in the illustration), those closest to the nut, are indicated with quarter-tone notation.

indicates a finger placement slightly lower than where Bb would be.

 indicates finger placement slightly higher than where A would be.

 indicates finger placement slightly lower than F.

 indicates finger placement slightly higher than E.

 indicates finger placement slightly higher than F#.

Table 2

These are not exact notations; you have to find the placement by finding the note (shown in the staff above).

There is a wonderful piece by John Luther Adams entitled *Three High Places (in memory of Gordon Wright)* (2007) for solo violin that uses only open strings and natural harmonics.

write your own

Chapter 2: Rhythm

THOUGHTS

Rhythm is the most essential element of music. There is a great deal of music without defined pitch, or where pitch is relatively unimportant, but there is no music without rhythm.

Rhythm is, essentially, organized time and consists of two aspects:

1. The underlying rhythmic structure
2. Sounds (and silence) in the context of that structure

The relationship between sounds and structure varies. It might be obvious, as in a march or dance, or it may be shifting and apparently indirect, as in a cadenza for a concerto, some free jazz, or avant-garde music.

Nevertheless, we create music in time by placing sound within a rhythmic structure.

Rhythmic Structure

Beat

The foundation is pulse or beat. This beat will proceed at a certain rate. This rate may be steady or unsteady, may get faster or slower; it may be deep in the background. But it is there.

Division of beat

The beat is divided and subdivided. Most commonly, the beat is divided by multiples of two; still common, but less so, is division by multiples of three. Division into five, seven, and higher occurs, but less often.

Occasionally, regular division is suspended within a beat. Chopin, for instance, wrote music with this effect in mind, and this free subdivision can be very effective in improvisation.

Meters

Beats are grouped to create measures, the grouping indicated by meter (4/4, 3/4, etc.). Four beats per measure is most common (which is why it is called common time), with three not far behind. Often these groupings are clarified by emphasis on the first note of the measure and the first note of subgroupings within the measure. This helps clarify the hierarchy of beats within the measure.

Measures with more than four beats are often thought of as comprising several groups of two and three beats. For example, $7 = 2 + 2 + 3$, can be felt as a three-beat measure, the third beat being $3/2$ times the length of the first and second. These "limping" meters are common in Eastern European music. They make excellent bases for improvisation.

Phrases

Measures are grouped to create phrases. Particularly in classical music, phrase length can vary tremendously. Bach for instance wrote long phrases arching far beyond four measures. In western popular music and jazz, however, the four-bar phrase is king. In fact, if the reader aspires to play jazz, one of the first things to do is to develop the ability to hang on to a four-bar phrase no matter what. When studying a jazz tune that is not already written four bars per line, it helps to re-copy to facilitate playing four-bar phrases.

Phrases are almost always grouped in pairs, like question-and-answer, or like a two-clause sentence with a comma, then a period.

Form

Phrases are grouped in hierarchical fashion to create larger forms. The awareness of how phrases make up a piece is essential for organizing practice as well as for effective improvisation.

For improvising with other people, it is essential to have a firm concept of the form you are working from. As shorthand, sections within a larger form may be indicated by letters. Much fiddle music, for example, is in the form AABB: a repeated eight- (4 + 4) bar phrase (AA) then another repeated eight-bar phrase (BB). Another very common song form is AABA. This pattern is common in jazz standards and shows up in classical music in the minuet or scherzo movements of sonatas (including symphonies and string quartets). Some common forms are discussed in more depth in *Chapter 7: Harmony and Form.*

Larger forms are built out of nested levels of phrases, groupings of phrases, and movements. This hierarchical approach allows the construction of mighty structures, like the great symphonies.

Realization

The rhythmic structure is a matrix into which we place sounds and silence to create music.

Silence

Silence is extraordinarily important in music. Every piece is (should be, at any rate) framed by silence. Phrases are set off by short silences for breathing. This is natural for singers and wind players. String, percussion, and keyboard players must do likewise. (I find it helpful to actually take a breath before playing and between phrases.)

In ensemble, silence in individual parts is essential for letting other parts come through, like in good conversation.

Nothing can freshen up your improvisation like reminding yourself to pay more attention to silence.

Notes and patterns

Notes (and silence) are placed within the rhythmic structure by beginning and ending at times related to the structure in order to realize the rhythm and create music.

Notes and silences of varying lengths (using the beat subdivision as a unit of measurement) can be combined to create recognizable patterns. These patterns can be used as building blocks for improvisation and composition. Rhythmic patterns can also incorporate consistent pitch relationships to make them more recognizable. A great example is the first movement of Beethoven's Fifth Symphony.

Figure 23

Patterns can be developed in the following ways:

1. **Displacement:** A pattern that at first starts on one beat of a measure can be duplicated starting on another beat, or even on one of the subdivisions.

Figure 24

2. **Augmentation and diminution:** A pattern can be sped up or slowed down by using more or fewer multiples of the basic subdivision.

Figure 25

Bach used this technique extensively in his development of fugue subjects.

3. Patterns can also run **backwards**, but I don't believe this is clearly audible. I would consider this one way to generate new, but related, patterns.

When improvising, it is not necessary to apply these techniques rigidly. The pattern can be reinterpreted more or less strictly depending on what the music of the moment demands.

Poly-rhythms

A fascinating subset of the use of patterns is poly-rhythms: playing two different subdivisions of the beat or measure simultaneously. See Figure 26, on page 42, below, for examples and how to realize them.

Articulation

Finally, notes are articulated in many ways to actually express the rhythm. These include:

Placement relative to the beat (behind or ahead of the beat)

o   Accents

o   Dynamics

o   Slurs

o   Ornaments such as vibrato and glissando

From these few elements spring infinite possibilities.

In order to work on rhythm, we take the elements discussed above one at a time in order to put them back together with deeper understanding and stronger skills. In working with the parameters below, start slowly and work mechanically. As you become comfortable, allow yourself more freedom, and bring in other elements such as pitch, articulation, dynamics, and expression.

Remind yourself to feel what you are playing and play with intent, in order to move from exercise to musical expression.

Rhythmic structure

For all of these rhythm exercises, use any of the following means to create sound:

o Clapping hands

o Pizzicato

o Bow an open string

o Bouncing bow

For notes, use:

1. Open strings

2. Whatever you are working on in *Chapter 1: Pitch.*

3. Free choice of notes

No matter what you use to generate sound, it helps a great deal to keep your knees bent, breathe, and allow yourself to move to the rhythm.

Beat

Practice playing precisely with a metronome at a wide range of tempi.

The goal here is to play so precisely that you can't hear the metronome. Since most of us (myself included) have an issue with rushing, it is helpful to pick a tempo, then ratchet downward step by step.

o Turn the metronome on to silent, with only a flashing light. Play (using the methods listed above), close your eyes for several beats. Open them again to see if you are still on. Slowly increase the number of beats played with eyes closed.

o Put the metronome on the slowest setting and practice playing free rhythms in between, but land precisely on the beat.

Division of beat

Take out flashcards with the numbers 1 through 6 (or through 7 if you are adventurous). Pick a card and practice that number of divisions.

Patterns

It is neither necessary nor possible to study every possible pattern. The idea is just to work on a variety of patterns. Write your own patterns. Then you will have your own unique collection of rhythm patterns.

Write a short rhythmic pattern.

1. Start it at any beat and subdivision of the measure you are working in.
2. Augment it by two, three times its subdivisions.

3. Divide it by two, three, four.

4. Play starting on other beats, between beats.

Poly-rhythms

Learn each of the poly-rhythms in Figure 26. If you are really ambitious, work out the poly-rhythms against seven.

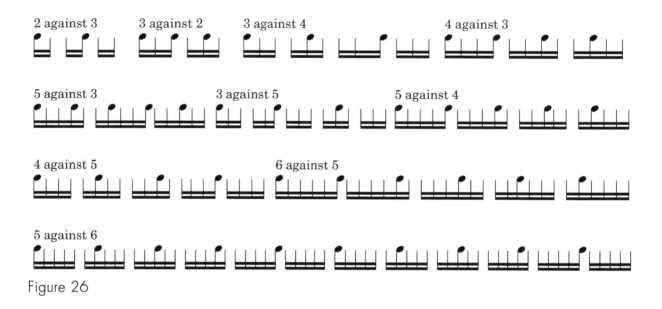

Figure 26

Rhythm scales

Drummers play rhythm scales to solidify their sense of subdivision. One of the best ways to do these is with a bouncing bow. Feel for the inertia of the bow to help you play evenly. Start with open strings, then move to scale material.

Play a rhythmic scale, with metronome, moving smoothly and accurately from rhythm to rhythm. Figure 27 contains two relatively simple rhythm scales.

Figure 27

More adventurous rhythmic explorers can include more complex groupings. Here is a list of rhythms in order of increased speed. To create a rhythmic scale, play in increasing then decreasing speed to the same pulse.

number of notes played	1	7	6	5	4	7	3	5	7	2	7	5	3	7	4	5	7
within this number of beats	1	6	5	4	3	5	2	3	4	1	3	2	1	2	1	1	1

Table 3

Meters

Take out flashcards with the numbers 1 through 6 (or through 7 if you are adventurous). Pick a card and practice measures with that number of beats. Some metronomes can be programmed with odd meters (e.g., Dr. Beat). If you don't have such a metronome, then you will simply have to keep track.

Konnakol

South Indian music has a rich system of articulating complex rhythms called Konnakol. A full discussion is beyond the range of this book, but the syllables used to sing rhythms would be useful for anyone wishing to improve mastery of rhythm.

Number of subdivisions	Syllables (note, there are other ways to spell these)
2	ta ka
3	ta ki ta
4	ta ka di mi
5	ta di gi ni du
6	ta ki ta ta ki ta
7	ta ki ta ta ka di mi, or ta ka di mi ta ki ta, or ta di gi ni du ta ka

Table 4

In Konnakol, these syllables are combines with a series of hand claps to create complex relationships among subdivisions and meters. The book *You Can Ta Ka*

Dim Mi This! by Todd Isler is a clear, concise primer on this wonderful world of rhythmic exploration.

Articulation

Now revisit these exercises, and include as many of the following as you can:

1. Accents
2. Slurs
3. Ornaments such as vibrato and glissando

Form

Although form is played out in time and therefore can be thought of as rhythm on a larger scale, this subject is addressed in *Chapter 7: Harmony and Form.*

All of these exercises will repay many revisits. If you can do all of these, you are a master of rhythm.

write your own

Chapter 3: Dynamics

THOUGHTS

This chapter mainly serves as a reminder to pay attention to dynamics: increase your dynamic range and use dynamics musically.

One of Ludwig Van Beethoven's many contributions was the written use of dynamics as a means of expression. Since dynamics are an important means of expressing form, this ties expression to form: the moment is tied to the whole.

When playing solo Bach, for instance, the dynamics are (with a few exceptions) not written. To properly execute dynamics, you must understand the structure.

None of us is Beethoven, but we can follow his lead: use dynamic contrast consciously and intelligently.

It will make your music bigger.

WHAT TO DO

These suggestions can be applied to almost anything you are working on: open strings, scales, improvisations, written pieces.

1. Just remind yourself: "Oh, yes, dynamics," and be more conscious of opportunities to use dynamics more clearly.

2. Work to increase your dynamic range, either on relatively simple material such as scales, or improvise:

    a. Play louder by playing much closer to the bridge, allowing more weight through the bow, and using a powerful flow with the bow arm. Use the whole bow.

    b. Play softer by lightening up and finding that perfect distance between bow and bridge.

3. Soft or loud, always make a beautiful sound.

4. Work with the smaller time-scale dynamics: accents and little swells. You can always tell a chamber music player by his exquisite control of dynamics.

Chapter 4: Left Hand

The left hand determines pitch on the violin, and this issue is addressed in *Chapter 1: Pitch*, with extensive material for improvisation. There are myriad books with left-hand exercises for the violin. This book is not intended as a substitute for these. The focus of this chapter is a physical approach to the left hand.

These exercises are worth revisiting at any stage of development.

Shifting and vibrato are minefields, probably the source of 90% of tension problems on the violin.

Geminiani grip

I give this exercise to beginning students, but it would benefit anyone.

Figure 28

Place the fingers as shown, starting with the fourth.

Wriggle the thumb up and down the fingerboard to release tension. Release all tension, except that required to keep the fingers well-formed and active.

When lifting the fingers do so with alacrity, but not at a fast tempo. There is a benefit to holding them in place as well as lifting. Drop them heavily, like stones. The fingers should feel as if they are either up, or down, but spend no time in the middle.

1. Lift and drop each finger at a time several times, starting with the fourth.

2. Lift and drop each pair of fingers (i.e., 2 with 4, 1 with 3, 2 with 3, 1 with 4).

3. Lift each pair; while dropping, simultaneously lift the opposite pair.

Stretching

Place the hand in fourth position, with the heel of the palm comfortably on the bout.

1. Stretch the first finger back as far as it will go (first position), back and forth.
2. Leave the first finger in its lowest comfortable position, stretch the second finger back to the first position, back and forth.
3. Leave the second finger in its lowest comfortable position, stretch the third finger back to the first position, back and forth.
4. With the first, second, and third in place, stretch the fourth up and down.

Ghosting

Here is another exercise that I give to absolute beginners. It helps with holding the violin comfortably during shifting, and is a preliminary to vibrato.

1. Place the hand in fourth position, with the thumb right where the neck meets the body (the saddle), with space between the hand and the neck.
2. Touch the string lightly with the third finger and glide up and down the string, keeping the thumb where it is and using it as a pivot.
3. While bowing, listen to the harmonics.

Shifting

If possible, shift on a half step. All the scale fingerings in *Chapter 1: Pitch* are chosen to shift on a half step (unless impossible).

There is always a "traveling finger." This is the finger that touches the string during the shift. When there is a shift from one finger to another, during a shift the traveling finger is the lower of the two, with one exception: when shifting from both a higher finger to a lower finger and a higher position to a lower position, then the traveling finger is the higher finger.

If these rules are followed, it should be possible to shift relatively slowly, yet cleanly. The shift should be executed with a simple arm motion in a speed relative to the tempo—never rushed.

It is also extremely helpful to play all the notes in the positions on either side of the shift to make sure the shift is truly from position to position, maintaining the form of the hand and fingers.

The major challenge in shifting is shifting downwards in or into positions below the fourth. This is because, in shifting downward, the arm moves away from the body, pulling the violin out of its resting place on the collarbone. Among the high positions, the thumb stays in the same place, which helps hold the violin in place, but once the thumb leaves the saddle (where the fingerboard meets the body), the hand and arm pull the violin from out of its resting place. Clutching with the shoulder is a poor way to address this problem for two reasons:

1. It creates tension in the neck and shoulders.
2. If the shoulder contacts the back of the violin, it significantly muffles the sound.

What to do?

The best solution to this problem is to anticipate the shift by a slight adjustment of the thumb into the new (lower) position, which helps pull the hand and arm as a unit into position for the shift. For shifting upward, move the fingers, hand, and arm as a single unit towards your body.

Below is an exercise that uses harmonics because shifts must be done with the lightest contact between the finger and string. The exercise is written only on the D string (for ease of notation), but play it on all strings. Choose a string with the flashcards (1, 5 and 9 for E string, etc.). Practice one finger in any session; choose a finger with the flashcards in the same way. For every downward shift, anticipate by first moving the thumb to the new position, and use it to help pull the thumb into the new position.

Figure 29

Note that 🎼 ♩ results in the same note as 🎼 ♯♩ which is 🎼 ♯𝅝

Practice shifts as slow glissandi, connecting the positions as much as possible. To practice all shifts, play a bow for the note, a bow for the shift, a bow for the note (as written in Figure 29).

54

Vibrato

Vibrato causes more tension, bad intonation, and lack of proper tone production than almost anything else in violin technique. That being said, it can also be a wonderful source of character, tone color, and expression. One of the first things one notices when listening to a violinist is vibrato.

Think of vibrato as a means of intelligent tonal enhancement, rather as an automatic default. It is useful to think of the bow as being primarily responsible for tone. Think of the vibrato being pulled out of the string by the bow.

One can generate vibrato from the arm or from the wrist (or a combination). I have found that using the arm results in more even vibrato between the fingers and less interference with the operation of the fingers.

I strongly recommend conventionally classically trained violinists to experiment with abandoning vibrato entirely, particularly when improvising and when playing pre-Romantic music. Although vibrato is used in jazz and pre-Classical music, the use is so different from the constant, frenetic vibrato one hears so often, that one must abandon vibrato altogether in order to approach it afresh.

write your own

Chapter 5: Right Hand

The right hand with the bow is the primary way that we create sound in time, as discussed in the *Chapter 2: Rhythm.* However, this chapter focuses on the physical use of the bow and bow hand. This chapter cannot be an exhaustive treatise on the bow. In fact, I do not even address the fundamental issue of holding the bow, since there are several approaches; why should I think that mine is the only one? However, the concepts and exercises here should be useful with any bow hold.

Bow proportion

"Where am I on the bow?" is a question one should always ask. And the answer should always be related to the musical intent: for instance:

o Up beats should almost always be played up bow (there are important exceptions).

o Fast passages should be played at where the right elbow forms a right angle, to avoid excessive movement of the upper arm. The exact location will vary with the player's anatomy.

o Spiccato only works at a point slightly lower than the middle.

Sounding point

The distance between the bow and the bridge (the sounding point) is crucial for tone production and dynamics. Generally speaking, move the bow farther from the bridge for faster, lighter bow; closer for slower, heavier bow.

To explore, play with moving the bow closer and farther from the bridge during one bow, snaking back and forth.

Slurs and separate bows

When there are unequal amounts of time for up bow and down bow, the player can wind up inadvertently advancing towards the tip or frog, and painting himself into a corner. In order to gain control over where you are in the bow, practice uneven bowings, in two ways:

1. Uneven rhythms: e.g., half followed by quarter.

2. Uneven groupings of even notes under a slur: e.g., three quarter notes followed by two.

Adjust the sounding point so that when you play more notes, the bow is closer to the bridge and farther away for fewer notes.

Choosing rhythms and groupings

Since there are infinitely many possible patterns, use the flashcards. Take out flash cards with numbers from 1 up to the highest grouping that you want to consider this time around. Pull two numbers at random, and using your pitch materials, play rhythms with the number of beats or number of notes from the cards. Adjust up bows and down bows appropriately.

Play:

o Open strings

o Scales

o Improvise

NOTE: write down your rhythm patterns on blank paper provided throughout the book.

String crossings

The hand describes circles (or ovals) as you alternate strings. It helps to imagine that you have a light in your hand in the dark. The clockwise circle that results from down bow on the lower string to up bow on the higher string is considerably easier and more elegant than the reverse. When choosing bowings for written work it can help a great deal to plan your string crossings to be clockwise. This can make a big difference, for example, in the solo Bach Sonatas. Conversely, it helps to be aware that special attention may be required where counterclockwise bow changes can't be avoided.

Bow proportion

When you change strings, the place where the string contacts the bow changes: when you move to a lower string, it moves farther from the frog and vice versa. Just being aware of this can be a big help.

Try playing poly-rhythms with one rhythm on each string.

Figure 30

This can be used to generate interesting accompaniment patterns.

Seven against five might be a little farfetched, but I included it for fun.

Calisthenics

I've described the below exercises from the point of view of teaching them to a student, but they are well worth revisiting for every violinist at any level.

60

The goal here is for the bow fingers to become strong and flexible "shock absorbers." This is particularly important for changing bow at the frog and off the string strokes such as spiccato and sautillé.

Collé

Place the bow on the string at the middle of the bow. Do not move the wrist or arm at all, as if they were in a cast. All motion is in the fingers. The first finger does not participate, but rather lies flat and relaxed on the stick.

1. By dropping your knuckles, pull the bow up bow, the thumb and ring finger doing most of the work. Imagine retracting your claws.
2. Hold this position.
3. Straighten out the fingers to push the bow down bow. Make sure the grip on the bow, particularly with the ring finger against the thumb, is maintained. A common fault is to go too far and push the bow out of the hand.
4. Hold.
5. Repeat.

This is a challenging and useful exercise. I give it to beginning students, but it can take a year before they quite get it. It repays patient effort—a few minutes per day.

When you are able to collé in the middle:

1. **Collé** at the frog.
2. **Squares** at the frog; move the bow in a square pattern:
    a. up bow on the string
    b. lift directly upward off the string

c. down bow in the air above the string

   d. place back down on the string

Then do the reverse: down bow on the string, up bow in the air.

3. **Circles** at the frog:

   a. up bow on the string

   b. circle down bow in the air, and place the bow back on the string

Then do it the reverse: down bow on the string, up bow in the air.

Pinky push ups

1. Put the violin down.

2. Hold the bow lightly in the left hand, horizontal as if to play the D string.

3. Lift the first finger slightly off the stick.

4. With the thumb as a reliable fulcrum, push down on the pinky so that the bow hits the first finger.

5. Let it drop back down.

Do the same resting the bow on the string and lifting to hit the first finger.

Bouncing bow

Playing with the bouncing bow (spiccato) after doing some of these exercises is a great way to put this strong finger flexibility into action. For beginners it helps to drop the bow onto the string and just let it rebound into the hand, as you would a drumstick on a snare drum. In fact it is a good idea to actually play with a drumstick on a snare drum as the feeling of dropping and catching into the hand is a little more obvious than with the violin bow.

The bouncing bow is one of the best ways to work out rhythms. I find that the inertia of the bow helps keep me in time. This is particularly effective with odd number subdivisions because you have to do the exact same thing but with opposite bowings.

I often use a bouncing bow for rhythm when improvising with others. Try it with just violin and a drummer.

Great circles

This is a way to get the bow moving through its entire range.

1. Start with the bow at the tip; move the bow straight past the frog, past your nose so that it winds up at your left ear. The right hand has to adjust to keep the bow straight.

2. Start with the bow at the tip; move the bow straight past the frog and up and around in a great circle, up and around, back to the tip. Keep the bow in a plane parallel to the bridge for the whole trip.

3. Start at the frog, great circle in the opposite direction, come in for a landing with the fingers acting as strong-yet-flexible landing gear.

Do these on each of the open strings.

write your own

Chapter 6: Melody

THOUGHTS

Melody is where it all comes together. Melody comprises all the elements explored in this book and puts them together in order to say something musical, as a sentence combines letters, words and punctuation to express a literal thought. Like sentences, there are infinitely many possible melodies. How do we make sense of such infinitude?

Because of the extraordinary range of possible melodies, all generalizations have exceptions. But generalizations may provide us with tools to improve our ability to create meaningful and interesting melodies. The only generalization that would be true for all melodies, in contrast to a jumble of sounds, is that there is coherence sufficient to express a musical thought.

Form

For melody, the paradigm is the human voice, though there are many excellent, even sublime melodies that stretch or even break that connection. Many jazz piano solos, for example are so fast, so chromatic and so wide-ranged that they are un-singable. The joke goes that in a typical jazz piano solo, the pianist is attempting to depress all the keys simultaneously. These are melodies, but we can say that the farther we get from a melody that can be sung, the less "melodic."

The sentence is a good conceptual model for melody. Both are generally modest in length (though length can vary considerably), with that length influenced by the need to take periodic breaths. The most common melodic form is: phrase, partial pause (comma, or half cadence), phrase followed by full stop (period, or full cadence). This creates a question-and-answer effect.

Figure 31

Rhythm

Melodies have some rhythmic coherence. They may be entirely one subdivision throughout (usually with the exception of the last note)—very common in Bach, for instance—or may use recurring rhythmic patterns. A melody may be strict in time, or exceptionally loose (as in a cadenza). Two examples from the Bach Solo Violin Sonatas:

Figure 32

Figure 33

Pitch

Melodies are usually composed out of a clearly defined set of notes, often the members of a scale. Many, perhaps most, melodies stay within their scale. This general rule is often stretched or broken, depending on the style of music.

Notes outside the scale are referred to as "chromatic" (colored).

Melodies in folk music and much classical up to the Romantic period usually stay within a scale. Mozart, on the other hand, used a lot of chromatic notes to great expressive effect in his melodies. He provides us with the striking example from his 40th Symphony in G minor, which uses eleven out of twelve possible notes of the chromatic scale.

Figure 34

Starting in the Romantic period and through the twentieth century and beyond, classical music and jazz utilize extensive chromaticism and wider leaps. One of the (many) challenges in improvising jazz is the extraordinary level of sophistication in handling chromaticism.

Intervals and melodic curve

Generally speaking, melodies may have any number of intervals in any order. However, to start, here are some rules of thumb for well-behaved, singable melodies in the spirit of pre-Romantic counterpoint. This is a good place to start writing or improvising your own melodies.

o Stay within an octave range.

o Start and end on the tonic; a different octave is allowed.

o Have a clear overall melodic curve: up and then down, down and then up, steadily climbing, steadily falling---with some counter movement within for variety.

o Approach leaps with a step in the opposite direction of the leap and step in the opposite direction after a leap. Note that this makes two leaps in a row impossible.

Once you have gotten really comfortable with these rules, break them one at a time to hear the results.

Singing and playing

o Sing a melody: whatever comes out. Don't worry about it, just sing.

o Play what you sang. If you find this difficult, try giving yourself an easy starting note, like an open string.

o Play a short melody, then sing it. Don't worry at first if you are accurate. Accuracy is worth striving for once you are comfortable doing this at all, but don't let initial inaccuracy discourage you. The important thing is to do it.

o Sing, play, sing, play in question-and-answer fashion (then reverse).

o More interesting, more challenging (and lots more fun) is to do this with a friend.

Rhythm, Pitch, Harmony, Form

Use the concepts of question-and-answer form, melodic shape, and use of intervals, and apply them when you are working the parameters in the other chapters.

Since the possibilities are infinite, the most fruitful approach is to focus attention on one element at a time. For the other elements, stay with ones that you are comfortable with. For example, if you are focusing on developing the rhythmic aspect of melodies, stick with simple pitch material, like the first four notes of a major scale. If focusing on pitch, use simple rhythms like steady quarter notes.

In melody, it all comes together.

Chapter 7: Harmony and Form

Improvisation on a set of chords

Another generalization to which there are many exceptions: in much improvised music, there is a set of chords (also known as "changes"), often the accompaniment for a song, upon which harmonic framework a soloist will improvise a new melody. This new melody may merely be a personalized or embellished version of the song melody; it may be something new, but following the harmony closely; or it may stretch the bounds of harmony and rhythm, while retaining a connection with the original structure. The latter describes modern jazz. The wonderful tension between a relatively simple (though often sophisticated) basic song structure and a far-ranging solo has created high art. Listen to what John Coltrane did with "My Favorite Things."

In doing this work, it is nice to have chords actually played to work with. There are several options:

1. Ideal: have a friend who is willing to play chords on the guitar, piano, or other instrument that can play chords.
2. Use a program like *Band in a Box* (see *Chapter 11: Resources*).
3. Imagine the harmonies in your mind. This is excellent, but challenging.

Chords and functional harmony

The discussion here is a condensation of a topic that can (and does) fill entire textbooks.

triads and more

Chords are created by starting with a root note then stacking notes, each a third higher than the lower one. The most common form is the triad, which is three notes, stacked, a third from one to the next: root, third, fifth. The type of interval that results gives the sound and name of the chord.

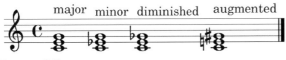

Figure 35

This form is called root position because the root of the chord is at the bottom. It's also known as "snowman position" because of how it looks[2]. Any note in the

---

[2] Thanks to Dmitri Tymoczko in *A Geometry of Music* for this elegant term.

chord may be used as the lowest note, but rearranging the notes into root position, it is easier to identify the chord.

In jazz and modern classical music, this concept is extended past three notes. As you continue stacking thirds, you continue counting: root, third, fifth, seventh, ninth, eleventh, thirteenth. Note that if you go this far, you have seven notes, essentially a scale stretched out in thirds. In jazz, seventh chords are the norm, with further partials thrown in for color. Unfortunately, the terminology for these more complicated chord types is not standardized.

chord function

Chords can perform two functions:

1. They have hierarchical tendencies relative to each other and to their key.
2. They have a color or harmonic pallet.

A chord's function is derived from the degree of its root relative to the tonic of the scale from which it is constructed. This is indicated by a Roman numeral, the number indicating the scale degree; major or minor are indicated by upper or lower case.

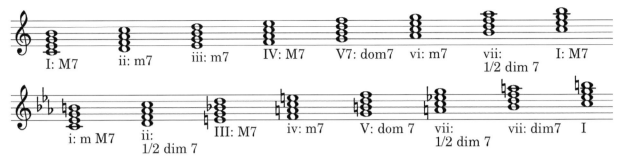

Figure 36

There are three chord functions that can be served by several chords:

1. Tonic

2. Dominant

3. Subdominant

The **tonic** function is predominantly served by the I chord, but iii and vi can substitute because they each share two notes with the I chord.

The **dominant** function is predominantly served by the V chord, most often in the dominant seventh (major third, minor seventh), but also by the vii° chord.

The **subdominant** function is predominantly served by the IV chord, but also by the ii chord.

(In minor, the forms of the chords reflect their derivation from the minor scale.)

functional harmony

The dominant function (V7 chord) has a strong tendency to resolve to the I chord (though at times this is thwarted). The subdominant function tends to set up the dominant function. Because of this, the strongest way to establish a key is with ii, V7. I is so strongly implied that it may be dispensed with.

This tendency is used to establish new keys within a piece.

As with all concepts in music, these basic concepts can be extended and realized in myriad ways to create the universe of tonal music.

Two approaches to melody on chords

There are two ways to derive notes to construct a melody—either written or improvised—from a chord:

1. **Scale-based:** choose a scale that is implied by the chord.
2. **Chord-based:** use the notes of the chord, plus non-chord tones.

These are closely related. The difference is more on emphasis. One should be able to think in both ways.

The scale-based approach can be a useful shorthand (more about this later), but it does not tell you how the notes of the scale differ in their function relative to the chord. So it is better to start with the chord-based approach.

Chord-based

To start, just work with a single sustained chord. As you progress, come back to this approach with groups of chords (see below).

1. Play the notes of the chord one after another as an arpeggio. To start, stay in a comfortable range.

2. Work up and down around these notes, not necessarily starting and ending on the tonic.

3. Add non-chord tones (more below).

This approach reveals a hierarchy: chord tones and non-chord tones. Chord tones are consonant with the chord and imply rest or stasis. Non-chord tones must be managed somehow: usually by resolution to a chord tone.

Moving from chord to chord

A great deal of the art of improvising on chords is choosing notes that create a good melody as chords change. There are three ways to move from note to note as chords change:

1. Stay there; hold the note (a variation being to leap an octave).

2. Move by step.

3. Move by leap.

Stepwise progression should be the rule. A **held** note that changes function due to a chord change is a nice way of tying chords together, or may be an opportunity for suspensions (more below).

Too many **leaps** can make a melody disjointed (which might be intentional).

Often, chords progress in such a way that their thirds or sevenths are a half step from a chord tone from the next chord. Using these active tones is a way to strongly imply the harmony in a melody.

Non-chord tones

One can play from chord tone to chord tone without any special consideration. However, moving to a non-chord tone creates a dissonance that must be resolved. Usually, the next note after the dissonance is another chord tone, but the resolution may be delayed further. The sequence is: chord-tone, non-chord-tone(s), chord-tone.

The non-chord tone may occur on the beat or off. On the beat gives more emphasis.

The sequence of chord-tone, non-chord(s), chord-tone tones may occur within a single chord, or may occur between two chords.

Approaching non-chord tones

As the chord changes, the status of chord-tone, non-chord tone shifts.

A chord-tone held through a chord change may become a non-chord tone, and demand resolution.

suspension

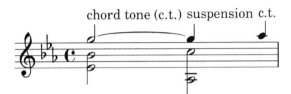

Figure 37

anticipation

Or, a held non-chord tone may be resolved before the chord change.

Figure 38

passing tone

If a non-chord tone is approached by step, it may be resolved in these three ways:

By **continuing** on stepwise in the same direction.

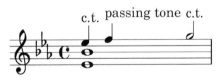

Figure 39

neighbor tone

By **returning** from whence it came.

Figure 40

escape tone

By a **leap** to a chord-tone in the opposite direction.

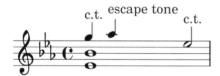

Figure 41

If a non-chord tone is approached by leap, it may be resolved in only two ways:

anticipation

By holding until resolved by the next chord. This is a fairly weak figure.

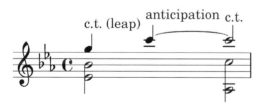

Figure 42

By step in the opposite direction. Appoggiaturas are almost always on the beat. Mozart favored these for their strong expression.

Figure 43

This may seem rather complicated, but it all makes sense to the ear, so the best thing to do is play these variations.

Scale-based

Commonly, these types of chords imply these types of scales.

common chord types	scale or mode
major or major 7th	major, Lydian
minor, minor major 7th	melodic or harmonic minor
minor, minor 7th	Dorian, Aeolian
dominant	Mixolydian, Lydian dominant, whole tone, diminished
half diminished	Phrygian, Locrian
diminished	diminished

Table 5

The scale approach can seem awfully arbitrary and memory intensive. And it is.

So why use it at all? There are two advantages:

1. It can free up your playing in a linear way. You see a minor seventh chord and you think, I can go all over the place as long as I use the notes in the Dorian scale. Nice.

2. After a while, you can see a group of chords and realize that they all imply a single scale. So for instance, CM, Am, Dm, G7 can all be played with the notes of the C major scale, tying the whole grouping together without having to fuss over each chord.

Like binocular vision, one must be comfortable thinking both ways.

All (but one) of the basic progressions in this chapter are in one key, which is the case for a great deal of improvised music. However, when one gets into jazz, changes often move into other keys, either momentarily, or even for entire sections. In some more advanced tunes, it is difficult or impossible to say what key they are in. The last progression in this chapter, Giant Steps, is a fascinating example.

Memorize each progression and practice it in all keys.

1. Play the chord tones; create a melody just using these notes.

2. Add non-chord tones that are members of a scale that the chord tones are also members of. Find several scales or modes that the chord will fit into, and use the notes of each.

3. Play with non-chord tones that are members of more complex scales, such as the Lydian dominant or diminished scale.

4. Experiment more widely with non-chord tones that aren't obviously part of a scale. Note that it is generally better to resolve these more exotic notes by half step.

5. Play freely and intuitively over the chord, just listening.

Sustain a single chord

o major or major seventh

o minor, minor major seventh

o minor, minor seventh

o dominant

o half diminished

o diminished

Alternating I and IV chords

After getting familiar with playing against a single chord, work with improvising melodies against alternating I and IV: two beats per chord in 4/4 time, as follows:

| I IV | I IV | I IV | I I |

This will reinforce the crucial skill of playing within four-bar phrases.

At first, pay careful attention to playing within each chord, but after a while you will realize that you can use the notes of the same scale (that of the I chord) throughout.

So, for example, in D major, start by using the notes, D F#, A during the I (D) chord and G B D during the IV (G) chord. Keep listening to the progression, but use all the notes of the D major scale.

Figure 44

Do the same in minor:

| i iv | i iv | i iv | i i |

Fifties Progression

This progression, affectionately known as the "Fifties Progression" (because it underlies nearly every pop tune from the Fifties) is also used extensively in classical music and jazz, where it is often used to quickly establish a short modulation. It is a very useful progression to master.

| I vi | ii V7 | I vi | ii V7 |

As before, start by carefully following the chords. After a while, you will realize that for the first three chords, you can play nearly anything in the tonic scale, as long as you acknowledge the final V7 chord by playing one of the more active members of the chord (the third or seventh).

It is generally better to avoid the tonic or third of the I chord during the V7 unless it is resolve downward to a V7 chord tone.

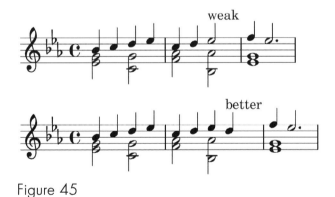

Figure 45

Blues

The twelve-bar blues progression is so fundamental that some people spend their lives playing music based on this progression. The blues is the wellspring from which spring both rock and jazz. It was also a major source of inspiration for modern jazz and continues to be crucial. Many jazz tunes are based on the blues progression.

Here is the basic blues progression (there are many variations);

|I7 |IV7 |I7 |I7 |IV7 |IV7 |I7 |I7 |V7 |IV7 |I7 |V7 |

Note that these chords are often played as dominant seventh chords.

There are several interesting characteristics of the blues progression.

1. It is twelve bars long. This is one of the things that ties together all the variations on the progression.
2. It is the only progression or style of music that I know of that conventionally ends on a dominant seventh chord based on the tonic.
3. Conventionally, there is a great deal of intermingling of the major and minor thirds.

The blues progression can be realized using the blues scale.

Figure 46

Note that by the time you get around to it, you can play pretty much every note of the chromatic scale. So, a good place to start is with a pentatonic form of the blues scale.

Figure 47

Like the "Fifties Progression" (I vi ii V7), be careful to acknowledge the V7 chord. If you do that, everything will be all right.

The blues is a highly idiomatic form with a rich history. For a classical player new to improvisation, attempting to play in a blues styles is probably a bad idea—at least at first. For one thing, the blues style violates nearly everything you have ever been taught in classical playing (e.g., "vibrato every note," "start vibrato at the beginning of the note," "don't play between the notes," "project your sound," "play what is on the page," etc.). To start, just play what works for you and don't worry about style.

The best way to get a feel for the blues idiom is to listen to such artists as B.B. King and Buddy Guy, and then play with people.

Rhythm Changes

After the blues progression, the progression most common in jazz is called "Rhythm Changes" because this is the chord progression for George Gershwin's tune "I've Got Rhythm." Here is the progression:

|I VI7 |ii7 V7 |I VI7 |ii7 V7 |I I7 |IV #iv° |I V7 |I V7 |

I VI7 |ii7 V7 |I VI7 |ii7 V7 |I I7 |IV #iv° |I V7 |I |

III7 |III7 |VI7 |VI7 |II7 |II7 |V7 |V7 |

I VI7 |ii7 V7 |I VI7 |ii7 V7 |I I7 |IV #iv° |I V7 |I V7 |

Note the form: A, A, B, A, each section being eight bars.

Here is a small list of the many tunes that are based on Rhythm Changes:

o Moose the Mooche

o Rhythm-a-Ning

o Salt Peanuts

o Meet the Flintstones

o Anthropology

The middle B section is called a bridge; this bridge was nicknamed the "Sears Roebuck Bridge" because it was so common. There is also a "Montgomery Ward Bridge."

Standard Bridges

Sears Roebuck Bridge

Here is the Sears Roebuck Bridge.

|III7 |III7 | VI7 |VI7 |II7 |II7 |V7 |V7 |

It is simply a series of dominant chords moving down by fifths.

One variation of this bridge substitutes chords that are a tritone (augmented fifth) away for every other chord. This results in a progression that moves smoothly down by half steps.

|III7 |III7 |bIII7 |bIII7 |II7 |II7 |bII7 |bII7 |

This substitution of dominant chords a tritone distant is common in jazz and is known as the tritone substitution. Note that the two chords share several common notes and put together create the diminished scale (see page 25).

Most of the tunes that use the Sears Roebuck Bridge use it as part of the entire Rhythm Progression.

Montgomery Ward Bridge

The Montgomery Ward Bridge is the more popular of the two:

|v7 |I7 |IV |IV |vi7 |II7 |ii7 |V7 |

Here is a small sample of the many tunes that use the Montgomery Ward Bridge:

o   Satin Doll

o   Honeysuckle Rose

o   It Don't Mean a Thing

o   Just Squeeze Me

Giant Steps

"Giant Steps," by John Coltrane, is a tune that altered the history of jazz. It is an enormously challenging tune—particularly at the breakneck speed that Coltrane played it—because the chords go by so fast, and because it never really settles into a key, so the progression has to be written with note names (upper case major, lower case minor):

|B D7 |G Bb7 |Eb |a7 D7 |

|G Bb7 |Eb F#7 |B |f7 Bb7 |

|Eb |a7 D7 |G |c#7 F#7 |

|B |f7 B7 |Eb |c#7 F#7|

The tune conventionally ends on the Eb chord on the last line, but this is totally arbitrary.

Here is a tonal analysis:

|(B):I G:V7 |I Eb:V7 |I |G:ii7 V7 |

|I Eb:V7 |Eb B:V7 |I |Eb:ii7 V7 |

|I |G:ii7 V7 |I |B:ii7 V7 |

|I |Eb:ii7 V7 |I |B:ii7 V7 |

Nothing but ii7, V7 and I7 in Eb, B and G.

This crystalline structure suspends tonality, in the same way that an augmented chord does. Like all progressions, it should be practiced in all keys.

Jazz Standards

If you are interested playing jazz, or just want a collection of wonderful tunes, buy the *Real Books* (volumes one and two). These books define the standard jazz repertoire.

Chapter 8: Accompaniment

THOUGHTS

Accompaniment is a challenge for the violin, because the range is relatively high. We can't really play a bass part, and we have to be careful to avoid interfering with the melody that we are accompanying by occupying the same range (see page 99 in *Chapter 9: Ensemble*). There are three situations in which we might wish to play accompaniments on the violin:

1. When playing alone
2. When accompanying a single other player
3. As part of a larger ensemble

Alone

Accompaniment figures are an excellent way to explore harmony and really get the structure of a tune down, when you are playing alone. Since you are alone, there are no constraints on range.

In this situation, accompaniment becomes solo.

When accompanying a single other player

When accompanying a single player, the problem of staying out of the way is reduced. However, it is still important to try to distinguish between the melody and accompaniment, keeping an appropriate balance.

Here are a few things to keep in mind:

o   The texture in this situation is pretty sparse, making it musically challenging.

o   If possible, play in a different range from the melody.

o   It helps to avoid the active chord tones (thirds and sevenths). Playing these notes will result in intonation clashes and vitiate the melody. Focus on roots and fifths. This leaves the higher partials for the melody.

o   It is your job to set the rhythmic and harmonic foundation so the melody can float free, so there is less opportunity in this situation for countermelody.

o   Short interjections during pauses in the melody can work nicely.

As part of a larger ensemble

As the ensemble grows, so does the possibility of duplication of function, and thus the danger of muddle. Your goal should be to contribute to the sound of the whole, not merely to play for the sake of playing.

Almost any ensemble larger than two will have someone on bass and usually someone playing chords. So how can you contribute?

o   Sustain notes to fill in the texture. Seek notes that tie from chord to chord or move only by step. Be careful not to cover up other voices, and try to find a range different from the melody.

o   Contribute to the rhythm with short offbeat rhythm chords (or double stops with several chord tones). Seek space where the other rhythm instruments are not playing.

o   A variation of this last is to use bouncing bows and notes of short duration to add rhythmic variety. Again, seek the holes.

o   Comment with either short melodic figures or horn-like blasts where the melody pauses for breath between phrases.

o   Double the melody in thirds or sixths. This is only really possible with a written melody.

Silence is crucial, particularly in larger ensembles. If everyone follows this rule of thumb, then everyone gets to contribute, resulting in a richer, more interesting mix.

The goal should be a transparent, kaleidoscopic, fascinating texture.

Here is a list of the kinds of approaches one might use to create accompaniments. Explore each in turn, then seek opportunities to apply them.

Bass line

Play the roots of the chords (most of the time).

Figure 48

When you are comfortable with this, add a few alternating and connecting notes to create a more interesting bass line. Stick for the most part with roots, fifths, and notes that lead directly to those notes.

Figure 49

Paul McCartney, with his melodic approach to the relatively simple (though quirky and sophisticated) progressions of the Beatles, offers a nice model for violinists.

This is the best way to start learning a chord progression, either alone or with a partner. It is less effective in a group where someone is already performing this function.

Broken chords (Alberti Bass)

Figure 50

Take the notes of the chords and play them one after another in short groups.

Alberti Bass is common in Classical period music; the superb second-violin parts of Mozart and Haydn provide a paradigm.

"Strummed" chords

Sustain double stops of chord-tone.

Use this with discretion and avoid the "active tones": third, sevenths and higher partials.

Figure 51

In classical harmony and counterpoint, one avoids parallel fifths. When playing inner voices in improvised music, I believe that it is more important to leave the "active tones" for the soloist, so this rule need not be followed in improvisation, since parallel fifths will be obscured by the other, more active, voices.

The "shuffle"

Used extensively in fiddle, the shuffle can also be done on three strings, alternating strings for a more complex effect. Note the accent on the offbeat.

Figure 52

Offbeat "chunks," too, are used in fiddle music. Play double stops of chord tones off the beat. Since the chords are shorter, the stricture against using thirds and higher partials is lessened.

More complex patterns can be developed by referring to the poly-rhythms on page 38. When the two subdivisions coincide, play the lower two strings. For one subdivision, play the upper pair; for the other, play the lower pair. The possibilities are myriad.

Rhythm

Using the same notes as described above, bounce the bow percussively, almost as a drum stick. Here the note duration is quite short, so higher partials are just fine. I find that dissonant intervals (e.g., root and seventh) work nicely with this approach.

If you are working with a drummer, the interplay can be quite exciting.

Countermelody and interjections

This is not strictly accompaniment, except that the purpose of a countermelody is to flesh out the melody. If interjecting (playing during pauses in the melody or solo line), make sure to pause during the melody or solo.

write your own

Chapter 9: Ensemble

THOUGHTS

The ideas in this chapter apply more or less to all music, though there are many exceptions. Exactly how they apply will vary. Some of these ideas don't apply to written music, for example, because you have to play what the composer wrote.

Clarity über alles

The primary virtue for ensembles is clarity. After all, why should anyone be playing if he can't be heard? Of course we should listen harder when playing in ensemble, but how do you create conditions that encourage listening, or even make it possible?

First, almost all performances are too loud, particularly in non-classical music. One of the most exciting performances that I have attended was by a group called Red Priest. This was a raise-the-hair-on-the-back-of-your-neck, sit-at-the-edge-of-your-seat performance, yet the instruments were: recorder, harpsichord, violin, and 'cello, the latter two with gut strings. Nothing was loud, yet it was tremendously exciting.

The common mistaking of volume for musical intensity, coupled with modern amplification, is resulting in a generation of deaf musicians. This is a completely unnecessary tragedy.

The key to clarity in ensemble is to understand the musical functions or roles performed by the members of the ensemble. These roles shift during a performance, and clarifying those shifts can contribute a great deal to drama and excitement. Another way to think of this is that a piece of music is like an ecosystem, with interlocking, mutually-beneficial roles. The system works best when it is clear who is doing what.

We clarify these roles in two ways: by dynamics and by frequency range. Nearly always, there is a part to be brought out with the rest supporting. This relationship may persist through an entire piece of music, as in an accompanied song, or may shift from moment to moment, as in a fugue or madrigal. This clarification must be accomplished by the supporting players adjusting their dynamics downward relative to the primary role.

Clarity can only be achieved by the supporting players adjusting their dynamics downward relative to the primary role.

The human hearing system has a remarkable ability to distinguish streams of sound, which is why, for example, we can converse in a noisy room. Two elements help us to sort out sound into distinct streams: frequency range and location. So in music, it is helpful to have instruments defined both by frequency range and location. When these are clear, we can delight in music of the most extraordinary complexity, even an entire symphony orchestra.

In addition to the evil of excessive loudness, amplification obliterates location by taking instruments that are dispersed just enough in space to hear them as separate voices and channeling them into a single stream that is rebroadcast through loudspeakers. This approach takes a three-dimensional soundscape and irons it flat.

The roles

The following description is not universal, but it is sufficiently widespread to be useful, even if the exact realization varies. Here are roles, arranged roughly from low to high:

o Bass

o Rhythm

o Harmony (chords)

o Inner voices

o Melody

o Countermelody

This is a somewhat arbitrary list. Not all of these roles are always present; some players may serve several roles. For example the guitar often serves to provide harmony combined with strong rhythmic drive. An accompanying piano may play bass, harmony, countermelodies, and occasionally take over melody. The music of Philip Glass is almost all harmony (in a driving rhythmic context). Still, one needs to hear what is going on. With these caveats in mind, let's look at this list.

bass

Bass is the foundation of the harmony (even when harmonies are obscure). It may also be the primary driver of rhythm. If someone else is performing a pure rhythm role, bass and rhythm work together to create the foundation and heartbeat. Because bass covers up sounds at higher frequencies, it is particularly important that it not be too loud. In small, hard rooms, bass can be particularly hard to control. The answer is: play softer!

rhythm

Rhythm instruments at their best can create an inimitable, bubbling energy for an ensemble. All too often, unfortunately, they just drive up the sound level and wash out all detail.

Rhythm instruments (except for the rare solo) must serve the music. An excellent rhythm player is self-effacing. It takes a really good drummer to be better than no drummer at all.

harmony (chords)

Harmony can be implied very nicely with no harmony instruments at all, as in the magisterial Bach solo works for violin and for 'cello. Explicitly playing harmony contributes to tone color and richness, but harmony should always be the quietest member of the ecosystem, with lots of pauses.

inner voices and countermelody

Melodic lines in addition to the melody can enliven the texture in three ways:

o Playing parallel with the melody to enrich its timbre.

o Interjecting when the melody pauses. This helps carry the momentum forward during those pauses. This requires the ability to pop out in the appropriate moments, then back down.

o Playing a complimentary melody in another range.

melody

If the other roles are properly played, it should be possible for the person playing melody to comfortably play with his entire dynamic range and be clearly heard. It is okay for the supporting voices to increase volume to support the melody, but it is imperative that they radically reduce volume when the melody gets softer.

Commonly, ensembles will balance by increasing the level for the performer who usually plays melody. This can lead to volume inflation as the supporting performers increase their volume to match the enthusiasm of the solo, and so it spirals into an impenetrable din. The only way to achieve clarity is to set the level of the melody where it is comfortable and then for the supporting roles to play at an appropriate relative level.

When the melody shifts to other players, the same principle applies.

In general, avoid unisons. Composers do write unisons, but even in this case, one instrument should play the melody; the others are color. Never have only two players on a part. If there must be more than one, make it at least three. It is impossible for two players in unison to play in tune.

There are styles of music (New Orleans jazz comes to mind) where several players will play different versions of the same melody simultaneously. This is called heterophony. I must admit, to my ears it sounds like a mess.

Silence

All roles should seek every opportunity to exploit the possibilities of silence to the fullest:

o Start and end with silence.

o Melody: Breathe!

o Improvised solos: Breathe, take dramatic breaths.

o Supporting roles: drop out for extended periods to vary the texture.

Silence is essential to music.

Rehearsing

The principles here will encourage productive participation from the group and keep everyone's egos reasonably intact.

o Arguments are good, if they are for the sake of Heaven.

o The best and quickest way to resolve an argument is to just try the several ideas. It never hurts to try something, even if you think it's a dumb idea. While trying someone's dumb idea, do it in good faith. (Do I really have to write this?)

o Be prepared to drop your own ideas instantly if they don't work, or if there just isn't buy-in.

Exercises

Here is a list of things to try in order to improve clarity.

o Throughout: Listen!

o Clarify the roles. Look for opportunities to shift roles, and for players to pause.

o Each player plays through alone, the others listening.

o Each player plays through alone, the others softly clapping their rhythms.

o Everyone, including melody, softly clap their rhythms.

o Everyone play (including melody) at the softest possible dynamic.

o All but melody play at the softest possible dynamic. Melody plays with exaggerated dynamic range. Actually, this is pretty close to how one should perform.

o Play the entire piece at half the tempo.

write your own

Chapter 10: Intonation, tuning, and temperaments

In all my years as a serious student of classical music and the violin, including conservatory training, I was never exposed to the basic theory of intonation, though I studied music theory extensively.

PURE TONES

The sounds of most instruments are fairly complex, but we can think of these sounds as a series of superimposed pure tones (more on this below). When we look at a pure tone on a graph of time versus sound pressure, we get a sine (or cosine) function. For this reason, pure tones are called sine waves. See Figure 53, below.

This chapter originally appeared in: Christopher Brooks, *Architectural Acoustics*. McFarland 2003 (copyright, Christopher Brooks, all rights reserved).

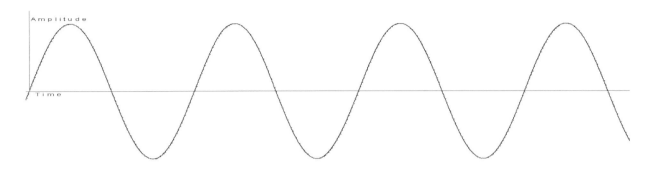

Figure 53

The frequency of a pure tone is how often per unit of time the sine pattern repeats. The unit is cycles per second, now called Hertz (Hz). We perceive the frequency as pitch.

Beats

When two sine waves with slightly different frequencies are played simultaneously, they interfere and create a composite wave that pulses at the rate of the difference between the two frequencies.

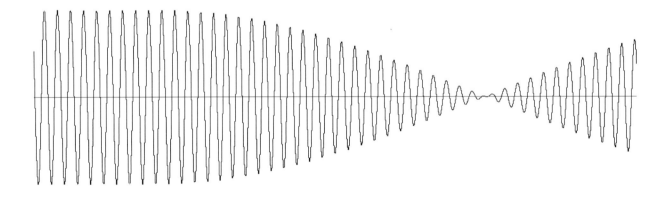

Figure 54

Figure 54 shows a 440 Hz tone and a 442 Hz tone played at the same time. The top figure shows the two tones closely enough to see the individual cycles. The lower figure steps back a bit to show beating when the second tone is introduced, creating beats that pulse twice per second (2 Hz), which show clearly as the cyclical growth and decay of amplitude.

Beats are what make out-of-tune intervals sound rough. They are easiest to hear with pure tones near unison, but they are also present in more complicated intervals. Beats are used to precisely tune pianos to intervals that are precisely and consistently out of tune. More on why this is necessary below.

Overtones

Musical instruments produce sounds comprising many pure tones superimposed.[4] These superimposed pure tones are called overtones. In musical tones, the frequencies of the overtones are in whole-number ratios to the lowest tone, called the fundamental. So, for instance, the middle C on the piano has a fundamental frequency of 523 Hertz, but it also contains overtones of 1046 Hz., 1569 Hz, 2092 Hz, etc. (or would if the piano string were perfectly elastic). The pitch of the fundamental is heard as the pitch of the complex musical tone.[5] The overtones with whole-number frequency relationships are called the harmonic series, and are the physical basis of musical intervals, harmony, and intonation.

---

[4] In fact, all sound can be seen as superimposed pure tones.
[5] There are some exceptions to this rule.

A musical tone with its harmonic series is illustrated by each of the "ladders" in Figure 55 below. Each "rung" is a harmonic, labeled by its frequency relationship with the fundamental, labeled 1. Spacing in the illustration represents spacing in frequency, using the logarithm of the distance, because this is how we hear pitch. The overtones weaken as they go higher, but the series continues infinitely (at least in theory). I only show the first sixteen overtones.

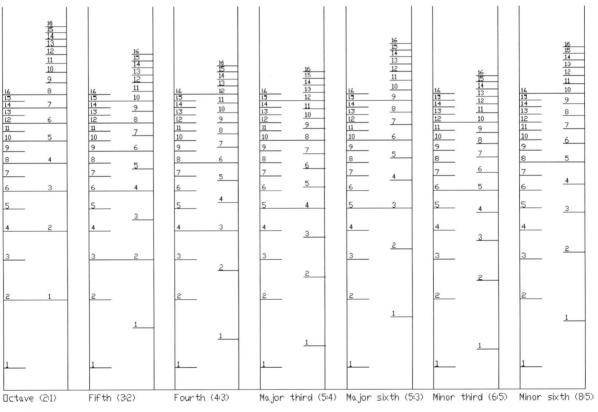

Figure 55

Figure 55 illustrates pairs of musical notes at the consonant intervals, in order of descending consonance. The consonant intervals are those that sound together, hence the name.

When two musical tones sound together at a consonant interval, some of their overtones match up. This is illustrated by the rungs of the ladders connecting. The most consonant interval (after the unison) is the octave. As you can see, every other overtone of the lower member of an octave pair matches with every overtone of the note an octave above. As fewer and higher overtones match, the intervals become less consonant. More consonant intervals blend more when they are in tune, but sound worse when they are out of tune. It is very critical to tune octaves or fifths precisely, but thirds and sixths are routinely altered by substantial amounts.

It is believed that Pythagoras (ca. 570-500 B.C.) discovered the whole-number ratios for the octave, fifth, and fourth. The ratios for imperfect consonants (thirds and sixths) were discovered by the Italian theorist and composer Gioseffo Zarlino (1517-1590).[6]

Whole-number ratios for consonant intervals							
name	octave	fifth	fourth	major third	major sixth	minor third	minor sixth
frequency ratio	2:1	3:2	4:3	5:4	5:3	6:5	8:5

Table 6

---

[6] Schwarz, Boris "Zarlino, Gioseffo (Gioseffe), "The New Grove Dictionary of Music and Musicians" ed. Stanley Sadie, 646.

Because of the unique prime factor theorem, it is mathematically impossible to play consistently in tune. The unique prime factor theorem states that any integer is the product of a unique set of primes.[7] You cannot reach the same note from a starting note by means of different consonant intervals, unless one interval is a multiple of the other (for example the fifth (3/2) fourth (4/3)).

Here is a concrete example that is easily audible on violin, viola or 'cello. Tune the A (440 Hz), D (293.3 Hz), and G (195.6 Hz) open strings by beatless perfect fifths. Then play a pure E (326 Hz), first finger on the E string, a major sixth above the open G. Make sure there are no beats. It will be lower than you think. Against the open A (440 Hz) this E will be very low, because a perfect fourth below A (440 Hz) is 330 Hz. The difference of 4 Hz is quite audible.

note name	frequency (Hz)	interval	frequency ratio
A	440	fourth down	
E	330		
A	440	fifth down	2/3
D	293	fifth down	2/4
G	196	major sixth down	5/3
E	326		
difference	4		

Table 7

---

[7] A prime is a number, greater than or equal to 2, whose only factors are 1 and itself. So 4 is not a prime because 2 x 2 = 4, but 5 is a prime because only 5 x 1 = 5 and nothing else.

This means that when playing the E on the D string as part of a C major chord containing an open G, one must play distinctly lower than when playing an A major chord with open A and open E strings. Few string players are aware of these discrepancies, which is why so few string players play in tune. The attempt to mask the confusion with heavy vibrato only compounds the difficulty.

Another example: If I go up from C_1 at the bottom of the piano keyboard (32.7 Hz) by a series of twelve successive perfect fifths (frequency ratio 3/2), I ought to reach C_8 seven octaves higher, at the top of the keyboard, but that is not exactly what happens. Let's do the math: 32.7 Hz x $(3/2)^{12}$ = 4242.7 Hz. 32.7 Hz x 2^7 = 4185.6 Hz. Going up by fifths brings us 57 Hz higher than going up by octaves.

Similarly, go from middle C (261.6 Hz) up by three successive major thirds to the C an octave above: 261.6 x $(5/4)^3$ = 510.94 Hz. An octave above middle C is 2 x 261.6 Hz = 523.2 Hz, a difference of 12.3 Hz.

What does this mean in practice? For fixed-note instruments such as the piano or organ a method has to be found for traveling from one note to the next regardless of the intervening intervals. The organ poses the thorniest problem because its sustained, pure tone makes intonation painfully apparent. Many schemes, called temperaments, for tuning the organ and other keyboard instruments have been tried over the centuries. The major drawback to most of these schemes is the fact that they tend to favor some keys over others.

Perhaps the most successful (though far from perfect) scheme is equal temperament, in which the octave is divided into twelve equal half steps. This is the standard method of tuning around the world for most keyboard instruments, though there are some organs that are tuned in some of the older temperaments. Harpsichordists will sometimes use other temperaments to suit particular pieces. Since you have to tune a harpsichord constantly, this is a wonderful opportunity to hear the differences in tone provided by the various temperaments.

In equal temperament, all intervals are distorted. Fourths and fifths are not so bad, but major thirds and sixths are too wide and minor thirds and sixths too narrow. Equal temperament really took off with the piano because the piano's decaying tone and stiff, inharmonious strings hide the defects of equal temperament pretty well. The stiff strings and the behavior of our ears require that octaves, too, are distorted by stretching. The piano is tuned sharper at the top, and flatter at the bottom, in order to sound in tune.

With other instruments, the player controls pitch while playing. Wind instruments are tuned based on equal temperament, but the player can adjust to match the intonation of other instruments. Because of their pure overtones (columns of air are not very stiff) and sparse use of vibrato, woodwind and brass groups can play very purely in tune. For the same reasons, they sound particularly sour when even the slightest bit out of tune.

String instruments are notoriously difficult to play in tune because the player has to stop the string with his fingers, rather than pushing a key or stopping a hole. This can become particularly precarious in the higher positions and while shifting between positions on the fingerboard. The open strings are the standard against which string players tune and these go out of tune as they are played.

Two other factors exacerbate the difficulty of playing string instruments in tune. One is the tradition of playing with exaggerated leading tones, sometimes called "expressive intonation." The other is excessive use of vibrato.

Following the practice of expressive intonation, the major third and major seventh of a scale are raised to lead to the next higher note. These notes are called "leading tones" because they lead melodically to the next higher note. Other similar melodic inclinations are exaggerated. For example, an F# in the key of G major is raised before a G to lead to it. This can work pretty well when the F# is not a member of a chord, or when playing with piano which tends to have higher thirds and masks intonation somewhat. Expressive intonation can also work well for a soloist, because it tends to raise pitch overall and make the soloist stand out above the orchestra. The master of this approach was Jascha Heifetz. His tone was like a razor cutting through and above an entire orchestra. He was also absolutely consistent in his intonation.

The drawback to expressive intonation can be heard on Heifetz's recordings of the Bach Solo Sonatas, in which exaggerated intervals undermine the consonant harmonies.

Vibrato modulates the pitch of a note around the note. Vibrato on the string instruments is an imitation of the vibrating voice. It is an intrinsic part of the sound of these instruments, and a powerful expressive tool. However, when it is used indiscriminately and too early in the study of the instrument, it can seriously undermine the student's ability to hear and play in tune.

Both vibrato and raised leading tones are expressive effects that have their legitimate uses. However, these practices should be built on a solid foundation of understanding the theory and practice of pure intonation. More widespread teaching of this fundamentally important and fascination theory would improve the playing of musicians everywhere.

Chapter 11: Resources

This list makes no pretense of being complete. There is so much more to read and learn. Web links are perishable, but I thought it would be useful to include them nevertheless.

THINGS

Blank music paper. This is one of the most useful tools you can own. There is some at the ends of some chapters and at the end of the book, but you will need more. Improvise on paper, then play what you have written.

A metronome. It doesn't have to be fancy. Use it often. Makes a great accompanist for improvisation.

SOFTWARE

Tone generation phone app. I use an app called *TrueTone* (pl.micwi.truetone). It's free and it works. Enter a frequency (in the box labeled "Hz"), and the program will generate several types of tones at that frequency. The sine wave is best for drones. The frequencies for each note are written on the flash cards at the end of this book.

Online tone generator (www.onlinetonegenerator.com). This one is free. It works.

Band in a Box (www.pgmusic.com) is a program that will play accompaniments in various styles. There is a large collection of existing tunes available, and it is easy to create new accompaniments. Tempi are completely flexible and it is easy to transpose, so one can easily practice a tune in any key.

LilyPond (www.lilypond.org) is the music notation software that I used for this book. It is a music typesetting program, which means no user-friendly interface which plays the note you are entering while you drag it onto the staff. Notation is entered in a programming language. It is enormously powerful and flexible, and—you can judge for yourself—I think the results are beautiful.

Bounce Metronome (http://bouncemetronome.com) is an online metronome that does the most complicated rhythms. For most work, an ordinary metronome will do (and is indispensable). But this tool can help you learn the most complex rhythms and poly-rhythms.

BOOKS AND MUSIC

Sonatas and Partitas for Solo Violin (BWV 1001–1006), J.S. Bach are absolutely essential for every violinist who has reached the level where he can play them. They are the center of the violinist's universe. I use the edition by Ivan Galamian because it contains a facsimile of the original.

150 American Folk Songs to Sing, Read, and Play, ed. Peter Erdei and Katalin Komlos. Every musician should have a permanent repertoire of pieces that can be played at a moment's notice. This book is a handy collection of tunes, many of which you may already know. These simple tunes form the basis for a full repertoire.

150 Rounds for Singing and Teaching, ed. Edward Bolkovac and Judith Johnson. This is another collection of tunes for the permanent repertoire. Rounds are wonderful instant ensemble pieces.

English, Welsh, Scottish & Irish Fiddle Tunes, Robin Williamson. Every violinist should have a collection of fiddle tunes that he can play at a moment's notice.

The Fiddler's Fakebook: The Ultimate Sourcebook for the Traditional Fiddler, David Brody is a large collection of fiddle tunes from various backgrounds with some useful background material on style, bowing, and recordings. A great source of repertoire for those times when someone asks, "Play something for me."

Hearin' the Changes, Jerry Coker, Bob Knapp, Larry Vincent was a direct inspiration for this book. It organizes the myriad progressions for jazz standards to facilitate learning and playing by ear. Well worth serious study.

Patterns for Jazz, Jerry Coker, Jimmy Casale, Gary Campbell, Jerry Greene contains an enormous collection of patterns for the serious jazz player. The challenge posed by this book helped me to come up with the flash card approach.

The Real Book, Volumes 1 & 2 is a collection of jazz standards, with the tunes and chord changes. These books help define what is a standard. Though most are written four bars to a line, some are not and would benefit from being rewritten to facilitate playing four-bar phrases.

Improvisation for Classical Musicians, Eugene Friesen is a fine book by a master 'cellist and musician. It covers some of the territory covered here, but from a different perspective.

You Can Ta Ka Di Mi This!, Todd Isler is a concise, practical, working introduction to the South Indian rhythmic system, Konnakol.

How to Improvise, Hal Crook is required reading at the Berklee College of Music for good reason. I particularly like his emphasis on silence.

Gradus Ad Parnassum, Johann Joseph Fux, translated by Alfred Mann. If you want to learn to write music, this book is the place to start. Beethoven and Haydn are among the many who have benefited by working through this text.

The Craft of Musical Composition, Paul Hindemith contains a thorough discussion of the theoretical acoustics roots of music.

A Geometry of Music, Dmitri Tymoczko is a fascinating approach to understanding harmony, including relationships among scales, that connects "common practice" harmony (i.e., Bach through Wagner) with twentieth-century and current practice.

Principles of Violin Playing and Teaching, Ivan Galamian is a comprehensive text on violin technique by one of the most influential teachers of the twentieth century. Itzhak Perlman, Michael Rabin and Pinchas Zuckerman are among his many notable students. It has been said that "Galamian could teach a table how to play the violin."

A Treatise on the Fundamental Principles of Violin Playing, Leopold Mozart is a fascinating and valuable source of information on pre-Romantic violin playing by Wolfgang Amadeus's father and first violin teacher.

The Art of Playing on the Violin, Francesco Geminiani is another source for pre-Romantic playing by one of the early, great violinists and teachers.

Before the Chinrest: A Violinist's Guide to the Mysteries of Pre-Chinrest Technique and Style, by Stanley Ritchie, a contemporary master of Baroque, Classical and early-Romantic violin. This book is based on decades of scholarship, teaching, and performance and presents the material in clear and readable fashion. A must-read for any violinist who plays music written before the mid-nineteenth century (which means everyone).

write your own

write your own

write your own

write your own

write your own

1 C 262 Hz	2 C#: 275 Hz Db: 287 Hz	3 D 293 Hz
4 D#: 155 Hz Eb: 156 Hz	5 E 165 Hz	6 F 176 Hz
7 F#: 183 Hz Gb: 188 Hz	8 G 196 Hz	9 G#: 206 Hz Ab: 211 Hz
10 A 220 Hz	11 A#: 229 Hz Bb: 233 Hz	12 B 244 Hz (tuned against open G) 248 Hz (tuned against open E)

THE AUTHOR

Please think of me as a resource. Any comments, questions, suggestions, arguments, recordings of your work, etc., etc, etc., would be greatly appreciated.

Christopher Brooks
925 Virginia Avenue
Lancaster, PA, 17603
cbrooks@creativeviolinist.com

I will endeavor to respond to all inquiries.

Made in the USA
San Bernardino, CA
04 November 2014